Evolving Spirit

A Common Sense
View of Christianity

Wim Kreeft

Hidden Lighthouse Publishers

http://fullservicepublishing.wordpress.com

Email: fullservicepublishing@yahoo.ca

Cover design by Jen Gerrior ©Wim Kreeft, 2014

Page design and composition by Vicky Anderson

Evolving Spirit: A Common Sense View of Christianity
First Edition

ISBN 978-1499653182

Dedication

This book is dedicated to my wonderful
wife, Joy, who has enabled me to
journey, question, wonder and be in awe
of the incredible world in which we live.

Dermott

May this provide
some 'food' for the
journey.

Wim.

Contents

Acknowledgements

We never live life in a vacuum. Our lives are intricately interwoven with the lives of the people that have crossed our paths. It is a blessing to recognize the people that have enriched our lives because they have willingly shared their wisdom and their insights with us. Therefore, I would like to thank the many people that have enabled this book to come to completion.

First and foremost, I would like to thank the people that have read, commented and encouraged me to continue my writing. So my thanks go out to Gordon Kerr, Dorothy-Anne Millsap and Dale Nixon. I would also like to thank the study group, which is the first group with whom I shared these ideas. To Ruth Dobson, Elaine Wyles,

Lloyd Somerville, Valerie Willock and Donna Nadolny, I give my thanks for your insights, your wisdom and your willingness to share.

Finally, I would like to thank the people that took the time to edit, challenge and review my writings. Donna Nadolny, Bill Ives and especially Lori Fowler I thank you for your creative insights, your kind ways of introducing change, and for willingly putting up with my recalcitrant ways. Last, but certainly not least, my thanks go out to Vicky Anderson who has been the midwife, allowing my writings to develop from conception to the birth of a published book.

Foreword

I have written this book in the hopes that the words, images and ideas, which are expressed here, will open people to the vastness of the Holy and to the awesome mystery of the Divine! Whether you never darken the inside of a church, or you attend faithfully, may you find some new understanding within the pages of this book. If you are wondering why your own children or grandchildren are not coming to church, perhaps some of the ideas expressed here will comfort you. For those who feel that the Church no longer has meaning for them, may this book provide new ways of understanding old stories.

First and foremost, however, I have written this book for my family. I pray that, wherever you stand on questions of faith, the ideas that are raised in this book will give you something to ponder and, in your pondering, I pray that these ideas deepen your sense of awe. This can only enhance your appreciation for the love and grace that is ever present in our world.

This book is not the final word. It is only my attempt to give you, the reader, a common sense view of Christianity and an inclusive understanding of our life on planet Earth. I hope this book allows you to see that the Spirit is always at work creating something new. May the following short chapters provide you with a measure of hope for the future.

Our Context

"*Excuse me,*" *said an ocean fish.* "*You are older than I, so can you tell me where to find this thing they call 'the ocean'?*"

"*The ocean,*" *said the older fish,* "*is the thing you are in right now.*"

"*Oh, this? But this is water. What I'm seeking is the ocean,*" *said the disappointed fish as he swam away to search elsewhere.*

Anthony de Mello

Introduction

Chris Hadfield was the Canadian commander of the International Space Station. In 2013, while circling the Earth for five and a half months, Chris spoke to many people around the World about the wonders and beauty of our planet, as seen from the perspective of outer space. His down-to-earth manner, his willingness to engage with people of all ages, and his ability to speak openly and frankly, gave his comments a wonderful vitality. Being able to sense the things that Chris was able to see, in just a very small way, gave us a new appreciation for this green/blue orb that we call "home."

Our planet is our home. As humans, we have never lived elsewhere. Movies and books can speak of space travel and life elsewhere but, until now, the only place of residence for human beings has been planet Earth. It has nurtured and cared for us. It has provided everything we need for food, drink, clothing and shelter. Its beauty has inspired us. The diversity within flora and fauna has filled us with wonder and awe. While it has been spinning around a star, within a galaxy in the vastness of the Universe, this planet that we call "home" has inspired poets and artists, challenged scientists and theologians, and dared explorers and adventurers. This is our world; our universe; our context; our home!

Stories

One characteristic of every race and people is their love of *story*. This is true, both for people of this generation, as well as for people of the ancient world. Perhaps the only change that has happened to story is the method in which it is delivered. The ancients relied solely on the oral tradition. But, after the invention of the printing press, stories in book form became more prevalent. Today, the most common delivery of story is through video or movie format. Each new structure or design only adds to the way in which story is circulated.

People still love to hear a good story, whether it is read to them or told to them from memory. Many of us still love to curl up with a good novel and allow the story to transport us to places yet unseen. The success of a Hollywood blockbuster is testimony to the love we have of story.

Story is also a wonderful tool for teaching and learning. Every generation has used story to give the generation that followed it a better understanding of their world. Some of our first insights as human beings occur to us through the sharing of the wisdom that is found in story.

The ancients would have used story to explain how the World came to be and how it functioned. Their stories answered the ubiquitous childhood questions of "Why?" and "How come?" which are posed by children the World over. Their stories were recited generation after generation. Eventually, what began as a story within the oral tradition, became a truth that was embraced, accepted and incorporated into an accepted body of beliefs.

Yet story was more than just a form of entertainment or a method used for teaching, it also gave each person an identity. The story told by one tribe differed from the story told by another. The story that was told *within* the tribe gave meaning and direction to each individual tribe member, as well as to the tribe as a whole. These stories would explain their religion, their world view and their purpose in life.

Story surrounds us; it fills us. It tells us who we are, how to live and what our priorities should be. It gives our life direction and meaning. It provides a road map and a guide for determining how to move forward in life. No matter what our ethnicity or nationality, we surround ourselves with story – story from our parents or grandparents, from our country of origin, or from our religious affiliations.

Yet we know that our world is ever changing. As adults, we are *not* living in the same story in which we were living when we were children. Our story is ever evolving, as is our very life. How have our stories changed? How have changes in our world brought about changes in the stories we tell ourselves?

Evolution of God

One of the most ubiquitous stories in our world is the story about God. Whether we use the name God, YHWH, Allah, or Buddha, or any other name, the idea of something larger than our own reality must have had some beginning. Most cultures do speak about "a god," or even "gods." For the purposes of this book, I'll use the term "God" as an all-inclusive description.

Human beings have been living on this planet for about seven million years[1]. We did not arrive equipped with a manual about life, or about the planet or about anything religious. All ideas, concepts, theologies and philosophies that exist today have evolved over time. So, too, has the very idea about God.

---

[1] O'Murchu, In The Beginning was The spirit, p. 9

Any story about God must have had its beginning within the annals of history. Let's begin by thinking about how this very story came to be.

Ancient people must have been in awe when they discovered that a broken bone can mend so well that the injured person can actually use their arm or leg again. They would have been astounded when they observed the healing of cuts and scrapes. Perhaps they were also amazed to discover that a cut will heal more quickly when certain herbs are placed over them.

On a larger scale, these ancient people would have experienced the devastation caused by a forest fire or flood. Yet, after these catastrophes, awe would replace fear as abundant life sprang up from the ruin and destruction. Today, we understand that fire actually brings new life to forests. It actually allows shrubs, flowers and various trees to grow. While they *are* intense and destructive, floods also bring much needed nutrients to the soil and an opportunity for new growth.

The ancients must have seen and wondered about new plant growth in places where animals had died. Perhaps they also noticed that dying plants nurture the soil and enhance new plant growth.

All of these things must have astounded and amazed the ancient peoples of the earth. But what is this force that causes new life to return? The awe-inspiring moments in nature; the force of the wind; the power of the waves; the destruction of storms; the shaking of the earth's plates; the birth of new life; the warm sunshine; the quiet of a winter day. All of these moments created for the ancients the idea of something greater, something life-giving, and something beyond their understanding. This something, which is referred to by many names, has evolved into the energy and force called God.

Some people see this God as a force that attempts to bring good to human beings, but only if and when those humans obey certain rules or regulations. Still others see this God as something that has the power of destruction. So they cower and cringe in their attempt to seem humble and respectful. Both of these extremes hinge on taming this creative energy within the Universe and on making it personal. Some religions strongly suggest that human actions will somehow placate this universal force.

When viewed as a life-giving force, it can be seen within every aspect of life. Yet, rather than seeing God as a living-force that exists within all of nature, we have created whole theologies about God. We have become much like ancient shamans, telling others exactly what they must do and think, in order to be in the good graces of this 'humanly-created' God.

This creative energy is not someone whose coattails can be yanked, or who watches over all of Creation with a grandfatherly love. Rather, it is a benign life-giving force that enables all of life to continually evolve. Diarmuid O'Murchu is a priest and social psychologist, and the author of a book entitled *Quantum Theology*. He describes this life-force as follows:

Life is sustained by a creative energy, fundamentally benign in nature, with a tendency to manifest and express itself in movement, rhythm and pattern. Creation is sustained by a superhuman, pulsating restlessness, a type of resonance vibrating throughout time and eternity.[2]

This energy, which is existent within the Universe, appears to gravitate toward, bringing forth life in all of its wondrous diverse abundance. It is not something that is humanly created; it is not an anthropomorphic being; it is not something that can be placated.

In the previous chapter, I spoke of "story" as being central to human

---

[2] O'Murchu, <u>Quantum Theology</u>, p. 209

activity. Many stories attempted to answer the questions that people have always asked – questions about how things have come to be. The idea that some deity is orchestrating the events on our planet has grown since the beginning of time. It has allowed some people to cease questioning and wondering. It has, in some cases, firmly sealed the door to further intellectual dialogue.

Early Stories

Ancient people created stories based on their experiences. Those who lived close to the ocean told stories about sea creatures and about the relationship they had with the sea. Those who lived in Africa told stories about animal migration, seasonal changes, plants, other tribes and even the weather. In North America, the First Nations people told stories about the Great Spirit, the Raven, the Trickster and other characters. The characters in these stories were teachers who taught the people about life and who explained the timelessness of events that dealt with their piece of geography.

The ancient Israelites also have stories that explain who they are. Their two Creation stories enabled them to tie their history to their understanding of the cosmos. The first story is found in Genesis 1. It speaks of the whole of creation, including the creation of all people. The second story is quite different. Beginning in Genesis 2:4, it deals with a beautiful garden, called Eden, and its first inhabitants Adam and Eve. Today, thousands of years later, Christians are still using these stories as a realistic explanation of the beginnings of our universe.

But these bible stories are not the *only* stories that deal with ideas about the beginnings of life. Every race and creed seems to have some story that relates to the beginnings of our world. In fact, the Israelites seem to be late in the development of Creation stories.

Michael Dowd is an American Progressive Christian minister and the author of a book entitled *Thank God for Evolution*.   He explains that much of history had already transpired prior to the Israelites even becoming a people.

Although none of this world history is mentioned in the Bible, no historian alive today would deny the following: Before Moses was born and before the story of Adam and Eve was written, southeast Asians were boating to nearby Pacific islands; Indo-European charioteers were invading India; China, under the Shang Dynasty, entered the Bronze Age; indigenous peoples occupied most of the Western Hemisphere; and the Egyptian empire's age of pyramid building had come and gone.[3]

Thanks to the Roman Empire and the Roman Emperor, Constantine, Christianity was given the ultimate position of authority.   The stories that

[3] Dowd, <u>Thank God for Evolution</u>, p. 11

are contained within the Christian tradition were accorded supremacy over other stories that had spread throughout much of the World.

When stories are first told, they have the ability to live and breathe. They are not confined or chained to certain theological or philosophical truths. Because they have been created by human beings, they can be added to, subtracted from, or changed according to either the needs of the story-teller, or to the needs of the listener. Yet this all changes when the words are written down. When these stories are placed within a book – a book people label as 'holy' – they lose their flexibility. They are written in stone.

Realizing that much history had already passed before the first stories of the Old Testament had ever been written, and recognizing that the ancients had no understanding of the complexities of the Universe, it becomes ludicrous to think that people would still claim that the biblical Creation stories are scientific fact.

Compare this with the following:

I believe the age of the universe to be at least 13.7 billion years, Planet Earth to be at least 3.8 billion years, organic life to be at least 2 billion years and human existence on the earth to be in the region of 7 million years.[4]

For millions of years people have been exploring, studying and pursuing knowledge about our planet, our solar system and our universe. Our knowledge is ever growing and ever

[4] O'Murchu, In The Beginning was The spirit, p. 9

changing. Thanks to space exploration and the Hubble Space Telescope, our understanding of our planet has changed dramatically in the last one-hundred years.

Shifts in a Story

There are major upheavals in the world when a new story is posited. People are reluctant to let go of their old story and accept a new understanding of who they are. Charles Darwin dared to challenge the common story about life and how it came to be. In 1859, he wrote a book entitled *On the Origin of Species by Natural Selection*. [5] In this book, he put forth a different story.

The response to Darwin's story, or to any other new story, is never based solely on knowledge and theory. Rather, it is based on existential awareness. We want to know how we fit into the bigger picture and what the future might hold for us. In essence, we want to hear a

---

[5] Darwin, <u>On the Origin of Species by Natural Selection, or the Preservation of Favoured Races in the Struggle for Life</u>

believable, acceptable, understandable story about who we really are. Darwin's story challenged people to see themselves in a different light, to embrace a new story. It took humanity out of its comfort zone and put it on a completely different footing.

Our religious history is all about the willingness to accept or reject a new story. Two-thousand years ago, the teachings of Jesus brought a new story to the religious establishment of *his* day. The teachings of St. Paul, which followed, brought a new story to the World that existed outside of Jerusalem. In 1517, Martin Luther, a German monk, helped to create a new story when he posted his 95 thesis on a church door in his home town of Wittenberg. Even though he was only attempting to bring about what he believed to be necessary changes to the Catholic Church, his ideas helped to bring about a new story about "church" and brought about the Protestant Reformation.

Today many people claim the Bible as being the very essence of truth. They fail to see that it is really only a collection of stories. It is not a book about history or science.

I wish to submit that the entire Bible, along with the sacred texts of other religions, is first and foremost a story and not a record of definite facts and events. In terms of faith, what brings meaning and integration to one's experience, the facts are quite secondary. It is the story (and not the facts) that grips the imagination, impregnates the heart and animates the spirit within (the spiritual core).[6]

---

[6] O'Murchu, Quantum Theology p. 120

As Jesus changed the way the Israelites looked at their ancient writings (the Torah), and as Martin Luther attempted to bring changes to the religious story of his day, so too we should look at our inherited stories through the insights and experiences of our world today.

The essence of story is how it touches us deeply within our beings. We cling to the narratives that tell us who we are and what life is about. We are most reluctant to let go of the well-known and familiar. We are reluctant to embrace new ideas and concepts that archeology, anthropology, astronomy and the social sciences have discovered about our world, our existence, our galaxy and our universe.

As scientists push back the parameters of learning, we need to adapt our thinking to the new story that is being put forward. Having to adapt to a new story is the very essence of living. As we learn, grow, change and develop, our story regarding our world or universe must change accordingly. When a person marries, gets divorced, has a child, or loses a parent, their reality changes and a whole new story emerges, which encompasses and explains their new reality.

Today, the story of people is changing very quickly. The Internet and, subsequently, social media have revolutionized the way people communicate and how they see themselves within the community of the World. The changes that people undergo will force them to come up with a new story about their reality and the reality of our world. Each person will have to find the truth that resonates within them; they will have to be in sync with the truth of the larger world. The story that people tell themselves will need to be a reflection of the reality of their life as part of the World in which we live.

Truth

Over the years, many philosophers have attempted to speak about truth. Every era, every generation and every philosophical school has put forth ideas about truth. Yet truth is elusive. It is based on the extremely finite perspective of humanity.

We do not live long enough to fully understand the meaning of our lives, nor do we have a broad enough perspective of the events of our world to put forward an all-inclusive truth. Yet for us to grapple with truth, we need to attempt to be as all-inclusive as possible. We cannot have one truth for religion and a completely different truth for science. We need to *embrace* all of the wisdom that has been given to us by the different schools of thought. What is learned in psychology, sociology, anthropology, history, science or religion should never be separated from other schools of thought. Truth needs to be a quality that is pointed at from every aspect of our world.

What is discovered in the world of science should enhance our understanding of our religion. What is discovered within the realms of the Cosmos should give us a greater understanding of our human condition. What is discovered within the realms of history and anthropology should shed light on the context of the biblical story.

There will always be diversity of thought. People will always look at events from different perspectives. No matter what 'happens,' there will be various interpretations of that happening. Societies, nations and people have experienced life in many varied and unique ways. Each race and each ethnic group has chosen how they wish to interpret and perceive life. Each people has a history. Their history defines who they are, what makes them a people and how they have changed over the eons. Yet it becomes imperative to interpret past events within the scope of present reality, allowing the knowledge of today to shed light on the journeys of the past.

Many people have placed holy writings, (the Bible, the Quran, the Torah, the Vedas, etc.) above the discoveries and insights of science, history, anthropology, archaeology and psychology. But that destroys the credibility of these ancient texts. Biblical writings should only be viewed as stories, which have been written by people who were attempting to point toward something greater than themselves, who were in awe of something they had either experienced or knew nothing about.

With the discoveries that are made through the use of telescopes, space travel and space stations, our understanding of our world has exploded into *new* understandings. If we attempt to corral the insights of our world into five-thousand year old thinking, we do a great disservice to our intelligence and to our history. Our religious understanding should never be allowed to become stagnant, limited to only what was known thousands of years ago. Rather, we need to be allowed to experience the awe and wonder of new insights.

Life improves when we incorporate the wisdom and truths that are found in other disciplines, and then utilize them to bring greater wisdom to our perspective of our world.

Science and Religion

Whether we are working in the field of religion or in a field of science, we utilize the same field of study - the same universe. All scientific advancements have taken place through intricate study, testing and experimentation in regards to the observations that have been made in and around our planet. Religious events are also grounded in this very same planet.

Our planet has been the laboratory for all advancement within the studies of science and religion. There is, however, a different way of understanding these two aspects. Science deals with objective reality, while much of religion deals with the subjective. In his book, *Thank God for Evolution*, Michael Dowd refers to 'public' revelations as having come from science and 'private' revelations as having come from religion.

Private revelations, as subjective claims for which no evidence for or against would be universally compelling, can only be believed or not believed. Private revelations, thus, cannot be known.[7]

Knowing the extent or the reality of private revelations could assist us in keeping an open and honest mind. An experience that lifted our spirit, or that caused us to see or sense something incredible, will not be an experience that is shared by everyone. When we fall in love, it is a most subjective experience. Our hobbies, pastimes and pleasures are part of our unique subjective personalities. Religion falls into the category of the subjective. It is not

[7] Dowd, Thank God for Evolution p. 68

measurable, differs from person to person, and is either true or false, depending on an individual's beliefs. This is all part of the private revelations, which make up much of our religious belief systems.

Public revelation is the work of science. Scientists put forth their ideas in order to have those ideas studied, refuted, debated, developed or enhanced. They are not subjected to the whims of other scientists, but are studied in relation to the empirical data that is found within the World. Dowd explains it this way:

Thanks to the scientific method, assisted by the wonders of modern technologies (themselves a gift of the scientific enterprise), public revelation emerges when claims about the nature of reality are based on measurable data and can be tested and modified in light of evidence and concerted attempts to disprove such claims.[8]

Science has helped humanity to more fully understand the wonders of the World in which we live. Religion has assisted humanity to have a greater appreciation for those very same wonders. Yet, because these two arenas deal with the same incredible realities, we need to be careful not to confuse the two realities. Karen Armstrong is a British author and commentator who is known for her books on comparative religion. She states the following:

Religions task, closely allied to that of art, [is] to help us to live creatively, peacefully and even joyously with realities for which there were no easy

---

[8] Ibid, p. 68

explanations and problems that we could not solve: mortality, pain, grief, despair, and outrage at the injustice and cruelty of life.[9]

The world of religion should be used to enhance our existence, not to explain the workings of Creation. Religious ideas can enable us to appreciate Creation more fully, but it cannot explain how the Universe came to be or how it is now evolving. Religion can give us an appreciation for the incredible diversity of flora, fauna and humanity, but it cannot explain how they have developed, changed, or mutated over the centuries. Religion has it shortcomings; science does as well.

Scientific rationality can tell us why we have cancer; it can even cure us of our

---

[9] Armstrong, <u>The Case for God</u>, p. 318

disease.   But it cannot assuage the terror, disappointment and sorrow that comes with the diagnosis, nor can it help us to die well.[10]

Science and religion are both wonderful gifts to humanity, each having their strengths and their limitations. Science enables us to see and understand our world more fully; religion helps us to *appreciate* that world.   Our religious experiences can be deepened because of the insights that are given by science. Our appreciation of the wonders of science can be deepened by the holiness with which we view our world.

Together, science and religion provide us with a deeper and more wonderful appreciation of our world, with all of its complexities and developments.

---

[10] Ibid, p. 318

Christianity Revisited

My point, once again, is not that those ancient people told literal stories and we are not smart enough to take them symbolically, but that they told them symbolically and we are now dumb enough to take them literally.

John Dominic Crossan

Introduction

The World, our home, has filled people with an appreciation for life and a deep desire to understand this complex and life-giving planet. When it comes to passing on information, the history of Christianity has had both a positive and a negative effect. At one time, the Church was the only place for higher learning. Many universities and colleges, newspapers and magazines, owe their beginnings to church organizations. The gift that the Church has given us is the possibility of hope for a better life, through education.

The negative aspect of Christianity within our society also deals with education. This occurs when people attempt to destroy learning by screening ideas through a very narrow understanding of life. This happened in Canada with residential schools. Rather than offering education for the betterment of the whole community, education was offered to cripple the Indian community and to take the "Indian" out of the individual. This negative aspect of Christianity also occurs when people attempt to understand our present world through the eyes and mindset of someone who was writing stories thousands of years ago.

Education should be seen as an opportunity to learn more about our world. It should never be a tool that is used to control others or to keep certain religious practices intact. Education should enable people to more readily appreciate the intricacies of our world, to question the status-quo and to prepare them for the challenges we face as a species, within our ever-changing universe.

In the late 1800s, some Christians became uneasy with the developments of science and the implications it had on their strongly held beliefs – especially their thoughts that everything in the Bible was factual. In order to define what they believed to be true about their faith, they came up with the following five basic fundamentals:

- the inerrancy of the Scriptures
- the divinity of Jesus Christ
- the historicity of the Virgin Birth
- the substitutionary nature of the Atonement
- the physical corporeal return of Jesus, the Christ.[11]

---

[11] Tickle, The Great Emergence. p. 65

Unfortunately, many churches still adhere to these statements. Thankfully, there are many others that recognize and accept the wisdom, research and scholarly insights that illustrate Christian teachings in a more dynamic light.

This section of the book includes a chapter that relates to each of the preceding five statements. I have changed the order in which they have been presented, to allow for a smoother flow of these ideas.

Looking at Scriptures

The inerrancy of the Scriptures is the belief that there are no mistakes, omissions or typographical errors to be found within the Bible. To believe this is to completely deny the very fabric of history. People have always loved a good story. They also love to explain how they, personally, understand a story. They love to explain how events have transpired and how their ancestors lived, loved, fought and overcame their many challenges.

Ancient writings exist because people have put forth their ideas and their understandings about life. The various writings in our bible was written by many different people. They were then collected and edited by many other people. Before they were written down, they had been part of an oral tradition, which could have existed for centuries.

The Old Testament alone was compiled over a period of about one-thousand years.[12] Yet, like most ancient stories, they were rooted in the oral traditions of the people, the Israelites. How long these stories existed (first in oral format and then in written form), before they were finally edited and included as holy text, is unknown. The books in the New Testament were written over a period of about fifty years,[13] but it was not until between the fourth and seventh centuries that the twenty-seven books in the New Testament were accepted as scripture[14].

---

[12] Brown, <u>The New Jerome Biblical Commentary</u>. p. 1037
[13] Ibid. p. 1045
[14] Ibid. p. 1050

The making of the Bible was, in itself, a very long process. It was written by many different people, over the course of many centuries. It was then discussed, debated and edited, prior to being proclaimed as 'holy scriptures.' It is very difficult, if not impossible, to assert that "all scripture is inspired by God,"[15] when humanity has been so heavily involved in the *development* of this book.

The central stories within the Bible are the stories about Jesus. Yet, if these stories are so crucial, why are they so different? Could they really be in contradiction with one another?

Did the birth of Jesus take place in a stable, as stated in the biblical Book of Luke? Or did it take place in a town, as

---

[15] 2 Timothy 3:16

stated in the Book of Matthew? Who was present - the shepherds or the magi? On the first Easter morning, who went to the tomb and found it to be empty? Did Mary Magdalene and the other "Mary" go to the tomb, or did Salome accompany them? Did only Mary Magdalene visit the tomb, or did a group of women go there together? If Jesus is such a central figure, why did his followers not record these facts accurately?

When dealing with sacred writing, or even when speaking of God, the tendency is to see something beyond our temporal setting. Rather than seeing the Holy as being present within our lives, we want the Holy to be *outside* of our world. Rather than seeing the Bible as a compilation of humanly inspired stories and writings, we want to believe that it came from some Divine being beyond our physical realm.

The sacred writings may have stood the test of time because they came with the label "scripture." But, essentially, scripture is a human document that outlines the experiences certain people had, which have been called "holy." The various writings that are found within the Bible should be seen within the context of history and interpreted according to the knowledge and wisdom obtained through the ages. This allows us to appreciate the metaphors, the imagination and the religious insights of earlier generations, while not allowing the message to be dimmed by literalism.

In regard to our thinking about scripture, there are some questions that should be asked. How many people today read these words? Are these stories still relevant today? Are there *other* stories today that speak about the Divine and the Holy? If we were to compile a new scripture, what stories would we include? How can we ensure that the nurturing, creative presence itself is seen as holy, rather than the written *descriptions* being seen as holy?

The Virgin Birth

In the ancient world, people who were considered to be important were said to have been "born of a virgin." John Shelby Spong, a retired bishop of the Episcopal Church, said, "Virgin births were a familiar tool in the ancient world to explain the extraordinary qualities of a leader."[16]   In fact, in most ancient religious traditions, certain people were claimed to have been conceived by the gods. A person who was said to be "born of a virgin" was someone who was important and who was held in high esteem.   They were subsequently worshipped.

Through the wonders of science, we now recognize the *reality* of birth. Like the births of all people on this earth,

---

[16] Spong, <u>Jesus for the Non-Religious</u>, p. 31

the birth of Jesus occurred because of human biology. People claimed that he was born of a virgin because of the esteem in which he was held and the honor his followers bestowed upon him.

The easiest way for human beings to disregard the teachings of Jesus is to claim that he is *not* human. By taking away his humanity and by worshipping him, we need not see his teachings and his actions in relation to the poor and the suffering. Nor do we have to understand the threat that he was to the Israelites in power – Chief Priests and Elders. We can whitewash the story by saying that Jesus was a sacrificial 'lamb' that was necessary for our eternal well-being. But this belittles the fact that Jesus was a peasant who stood for the down-trodden and who stood against the powers of his day. By crucifying him, they ensured that the rich and the powerful could maintain the status quo.

The claim that Jesus was born of a virgin also hinges on our understanding of the Divine. If the Divine is the very energy that has caused the Universe to come into existence, the very power that continually nurtures all of life, and the very force the early Israelites called YHWY, then the idea of a virgin birth speaks, not about the condition of the birth of Jesus but, rather, about the *effect* that he had on his followers.

Jesus in a New Light (or the Divinity of Jesus)

As we look back on two-thousand plus years of the history of Christianity, it becomes difficult to get a clear picture of the person who was called Jesus. For the past two millennia, people have made many varied claims about Jesus, within the biblical text. If we are to believe the literal interpretation, Jesus would have had to be super-human or, at the very least, he would have had to be an incredible magician. If Jesus was born in the same way as all other human beings are born, from the physical combination of sperm and egg, how can we begin to understand the reality of this carpenter-cum-world-changer? How can we begin to see his humanity within the scope of what was spoken about him?

We know that Jesus was an exceptional individual. Yet the problem for us today is in determining how to understand him within our present context. The possible solution for me came when I read the book, *The Spark*, which was written by Kristine Barnett about her son Jake.

At two years of age, Jake was diagnosed with severe autism. The family was told that he would probably never develop much past the level of a seven-year old. Kristine found the diagnosis difficult to accept. So she did whatever she could to ignite her son's interest, even if it was only a momentary flicker.

One night, she discovered that flicker of interest when she and Jake were lying back, looking at the stars. She could sense that Jake was keenly interested in outer space. So, when he was three years of age, she took him to an observatory to view the planet Mars. This was the first small step that they would take on a most remarkable journey. The following excerpt from Kristine's book illustrates the uniqueness of Jake's mind:

Then the lecturer asked a question of the audience: "Our moon is round. Why do you think the moons around Mars are elliptical, shaped like potatoes?"

Nobody in the crowd answered, probably because no one had the slightest idea. I certainly didn't. Then Jake's hand shot up. "Excuse me, but could you please tell me the size of these moons?" This was more conversation than I'd seen from Jake in his entire life, but then again, I'd never tried to talk to him about Mars's moons. The lecturer, visibly surprised, answered him. To the astonishment of everyone, including me,

Jake responded, "Then the moons around Mars are small, so they have a small mass. The gravitational effects of the moons are not large enough to pull them into complete spheres."

He was right.

The room went silent, all eyes on my son. Then everyone went nuts and for a few minutes the lecture came to a halt.[17]

By the time Jake Barnett was eight years old, he was speaking to professors at the local university regarding astrophysics. By the time he was ten years old, he was enrolled at that same university. At age thirteen, he was developing ideas that would challenge some of Einstein's theories. His view of reality allows him to perceive things within the universe and within galaxies that would perplex most of us.

---

[17] Barnett, The Spark, p. 88

It is my opinion that Jesus could have been someone like Jake. Jesus perceived the World, along with the people in it, in a most unique and wonderful way. Much to the consternation of the local authorities, Jesus continued to push back the parameters of his religion. He forced people to look beyond rules and regulations, to perceive the importance of caring for others.

Just like Jake, Jesus amazed people, even in his youth. Like Jake, Jesus was able to see the World differently. He allowed himself to function at a different level of reality. The story of Jesus speaking to the Samaritan woman reveals his depth of understanding in regards to her personal struggles and to the tension that existed within Jewish and Samaritan communities, as well as his ability to forge a new reality and a new hope for her, for the community and for his disciples.[18]   He, willingly, openly and honestly, broke the rules of his day. He had a level of understanding that transcended what we consider to be "the norm."

The Gospel stories show that Jesus had an ability to see the World in a different way. It is my opinion that the stories about Jesus need to be taken seriously and that they should be understood within the reality of our world. He teaches us much about life and about the way we live. Yet, as different as Jesus may have been, I believe strongly that he was an extremely gifted human being.

---

[18] John 4:1-42

Dying to Give Life (Substitutionary Atonement)

Within Christian circles, we hear the phrase, "Jesus died for our sins." The phrase is used often. It has become one of those statements that people no longer seem to question. This atonement is referred to as "substitutionary atonement." The author of John's letters writes: "Jesus is the full payment for our sins and not for our sins only, but for those of the whole world"[19]. In his letter to the Romans, St. Paul put it this way.

At the appointed time, when we were still powerless, Christ dies for us godless people. It is not easy to die even for a good person – though of course for someone really worthy, there might be

---

[19] 1 John 2:2

someone prepared to die – but the proof of God's love is that Christ died for us even while we were sinners.[20]

The idea that lies at the heart of substitutionary atonement is a carryover from ancient times. The Israelites believed that, if they sacrificed an animal in exchange for their sins or wrong doings, this would somehow appease God. The belief that a blood sacrifice was necessary to make us right with God seems ludicrous at best. How can killing an animal change the relationship we have with the Divine?

Yet early followers of Jesus, St. Paul included, attempted to suggest that Jesus needed to die in order for the rest of us to be "right" with God. Why does the murdering of one person two-

---

[20] Romans 5:6-8

thousand years ago make us right with the Divine energy that has given rise to all of life? Do we still think that making blood sacrifices somehow changes our very being – making us more loving, kind, generous and forgiving? Speaking of Jesus as a sacrifice diminishes what Jesus taught and how he lived.

If we think of life and all that it entails, we realize that death is very much a part of life. Every living thing is finite, having a certain beginning (birth) and a certain end (death). All living things die and, in the process of dying, they give life. When a plant dies, it decays and returns to the soil, becoming nutrients for other plants. When an animal eats a plant, that plant provides nutrients for the animal. When an animal dies, its remains become nutrients for either plants or animals.

Death and dying allows and enables the process of life to continue within all of nature.

However, human beings are slightly different. We *also* live and die for the well-being of others, but not in the same way that plants and animals do. We actually *spend* our lives in order that others may live. Every person exists because of the gifts of others.

I am writing this because there have been people in my life who taught school, developed computers and built homes. Some people have provided the gifts of electricity, heating and water; others have provided the skills that are necessary for editing and publishing. We exist because of the millions of people who have spent their lives giving to the greater community. In the process of spending their lives, eventually, they die.

But, thankfully, they have used their skills and their wisdom for the well-being of others.

Dying to give life also happens within our universe. On a very large scale, stars have died in order to give us life. Lawrence M. Krauss is a physicist and the author of a book entitled *A Universe from Nothing*. He writes the following:

While lithium is important for some people, far more important to the rest of us are all the heavier nuclei like carbon, nitrogen, oxygen, iron and so on. These were not made in the Big Bang. The only place they can be made is in the fiery cores of stars. And the only way they could get into your body today is if these stars were kind enough to have exploded, spewing their products into the cosmos so they could one day coalesce in and around a small blue planet located near the star we call the Sun. Over the course of the history of our galaxy, about 200 million stars have exploded. These myriad stars sacrificed themselves, if you wish, so that one day you could be born. I suppose that qualifies them as much as anything else for the role of saviors.[21]

The gift of life is the opportunity to share ourselves with the living community for the continued well-being of our universe. The life of Jesus was offered as an example. His offering enabled others to become the best that they could be. Indeed, he lived so that others can live more fully.

It is said that Jesus died for us. But it should really be said that Jesus *lived* for us! Jesus was a living testimony to the way life should be lived – nurturing, caring, loving and forgiving – of all he encountered.

---

[21] Krauss, <u>A Universe from Nothing</u>, p. 18-19

The Return of Christ

The thought that Jesus will return to this earth in bodily form raises serious questions about how we understand our world. It raises questions about what our understandings of Jesus and the Christ really are.

We have already discussed the need to see our world within the context of scientific understanding. We have seen that God is really a creative, nurturing energy that affects all of life. We have seen that Jesus was very much a human being, one who had an incredible impact on the people he encountered. Now we need to make a distinction between the *person* named Jesus and the *title* of Christ.

Jesus was a historical figure who lived about two-thousand years ago. He was considered by many to be an incredible person who embodied the very essence of what they thought it meant to live as God would have us live. The way he affected others was so profound that they referred to him as their "saviour" - the Messiah.

This embodiment of God-like qualities also enabled his followers to suggest that Jesus was the son of God because he was so close to the very essence of how they perceived God to be. In the Gospel of John, it is stated, "the Word became flesh and lived among us,"[22] This suggests that the qualities of the Divine must always be embodied within the lives of real people. The Divine qualities are never just an abstract that exists in some out-of-this-

---

[22] John 1:14

world place. Rather, they are the very qualities that we admire most in the people that are our neighbours, friends and family members.

To imagine that Jesus will return to the Earth in a bodily form dismisses the reality of his very normal birth, as well as the essence of his very personhood. It also belittles the insights of his teachings and the essence of those Divine qualities. If we speak of the return of Jesus, we should not speak of the return of his physical form. Rather, we should speak of the return of those Divine qualities that he embodied. It is those qualities that are always present in life - qualities that never die, but that live on forever.

During the twentieth century, we were blessed with some wonderful people who demonstrated the embodiment of those eternal qualities.

Martin Luther King, Jr. sought equality for Afro-American people and, in so doing, he gave hope and meaning to the lives of millions of people in the United States and around the World.   Mother Teresa gave hope to millions of people in Calcutta by insisting that all people are valuable and should be cared for.   By living the qualities of hope, forgiveness and kindness, Nelson Mandela gave hope to people the World over. Symbolically, these three people make real the biblical story of Lazarus being raised from the dead.   The work they did raised many people from the tombs of racism, hatred and disregard, enabling many others to be empowered to live whole and complete lives.

Jesus will not return to us in a physical form. But the qualities that he demonstrated will continue to live on.

When we see these qualities, experience this love, grace and forgiveness, we can say that there has been a resurrection of the Holy.

Church: Pros and Cons

The master's sermon that day consisted of one enigmatic sentence.
With a wry smile he said, "All I do is sit by the bank of the river, selling river water."

Anthony "Tony" de Mello

Introduction

Jesus lived for about thirty-three years. While he was alive, he had an incredible influence on the people with whom he lived, taught and shared life experiences. After his untimely death, people wanted to continue the work Jesus had begun. They gathered together to remember his teachings, usually in people's homes. Those early gathering places became known as 'church.'

The word *church* is the English translation of the Greek word, *ekklesia*, which means 'assembly or gathering.'[23] Over the last two-thousand years, churches have been the gathering places for people who claim to be followers of Jesus. They have adopted the word

---

[23] Achtemeier, Harper's Bible Dictionary, p. 168

Christian because they saw Jesus as the Christ, the Messiah or the Promised One of God.

The church has had many ups and downs over the years. Before the time of Constantine, many people viewed the Church as a threat. Romans were fond of throwing Christians to the lions. For the sake of peace in the Roman world, Constantine established Christianity as the main religion. Being the one and only accepted religion of the day allowed church bureaucracy to control thinking, theologies and development. This enabled organizations, like the Spanish Inquisition, to exercise power over people who may have been a threat to their idea of the Church. But to control the thinking of others is impossible.

In the late 1400s and early 1500s the beginnings of the Protestant

Reformation created unsettling conditions for the dominant Roman Catholic Church. This church, which attempted to remain as the one and only church, had already been rocked by early schisms. These schisms created Eastern Orthodox churches, which were rooted in eastern parts of Europe, as well as Coptic Churches, which were rooted in Egypt. The history of the Church is a history of a people that were continually breaking away from one group in order to form another group. It is a history of a people that wanted to establish what they believed to be the one correct interpretation of the person, named Jesus, and how to best *enable* that interpretation to be practiced in life.

While the Church is an organization that attempts to follow the teachings of Jesus, it appears to be hampered by its own history and bureaucracy. It is not the teachings of Jesus that become front and centre but, rather, what historical church leaders have claimed to be important and crucial.

The following chapters look more closely at aspects of 'church' as the human institution that attempts to remain true to the life and teachings of Jesus.

Tower of Babel

The following story is found in the biblical Book of Genesis. It is a narration about people having an idea about building a tower:

Throughout the earth, people spoke the same language and used the same words. Now, as they moved eastward, they found a valley in the land of Shinar and settled there. They all said to one another, "Let us make bricks and bake them in the fire." They used bricks as building stones and bitumen for mortar. Then they said, "Let us build ourselves a city and a tower whose top can reach to heaven. Let us make a name for ourselves, to keep us from being scattered over the face of the whole earth."

YHWH came down to see the city and the tower these mortals had built. "They are a single people with a single language,"

YHWH said. "And this is but the beginning of their undertakings! Now there will be nothing too hard for them to do. Come, let us go down and baffle their language so that they can no longer understand one another." So YHWH scattered them over the face of the earth and they had to stop building the city. It was named Babel, because YHWH made humans babble different languages throughout the World. It was from there that YHWH scattered them over the whole earth.[24]

Let's summarize this story. Certain people sell to others their idea about building a tower. The idea takes hold and then the work begins. Eventually, some of the workers begin to question the purpose and the plan of this building project. They cease to buy into the ideas behind the plan. They no longer understand the purpose, the dream, or

---

[24] Genesis 11:1-9

the function of this tower. The ideas and implications of the original dream cease to speak to their understanding of life, and they have no choice but to seek meaning for their lives elsewhere. They walk away from Babel.

It is my opinion that this story symbolizes what has happened to many organizations, including the Church. Very few churches function by themselves. Most churches are part of a larger organization. I am a member of a local United Church. This local church is also part of a regional organization called 'presbytery' that, in turn, is part of an even larger grouping called 'conference.' All of the conferences combined make up the General Council for the United Church of Canada.

As church structures become larger and more complex, the decision making process slowly becomes more centralized. In an attempt to be more efficient, churches and other organizations put the decision making process into the hands of fewer and fewer people. Churches still function somewhat autonomously. But too often there are directives from the higher branches of the Church hierarchy that dictate direction and policy for the Church as a whole.

When the people in the pew are no longer able to participate in the decision making process of the larger organization, they lose interest. Like the people in the Tower of Babel story, they walk away. Like the people who maintain them, churches need to be present and active in the decision making process.

Early churches were rooted within community. They functioned within a particular society, attempting to offer solace and hope for people, neighbours and friends, who were struggling with the many difficulties of life. Yet the individual church is not just an organization within a specific community. It can also be a part of an organization that extends to the whole country or beyond.

The role of the larger aspects of church – provincial, national, or international – is to deal with the challenges that are facing, not just a local community, but provinces, nations and people around the globe. In order to keep the Church organization running smoothly, policy needs to be put in place. If policy is instituted, people need to bend according to the rules and regulations.   Larger organizations need strong policy in order to maintain the efficiency of their business or church.

When policy is placed ahead of people, frustration sets in. Then, similar to the Tower of Babel story, people no longer relate to the decision making processes. They find new ways to exist. People need to feel respected, honored and important.   Placing policy ahead of people speaks volumes and encourages people to find new ways of being.

There is yet a third way that this story seems appropriate for the situation that is facing many churches today. Today, many people are well-educated. Learning has come both on a cosmic level, as well as on a microscopic level. People have learned about some of the properties of the Universe, with its thousands of galaxies, each of which contains millions of stars. They have also learned about the miniscule properties within the atom. The atom is made up of protons, electrons and neutrons that, in turn, are made up of even more minute particles. People have also learned about the history of our world, both in years, as well as in events. All of this learning has given people a wonderful new perspective.

Imagine the surprise on the face of a person coming into a church. It would sound incredulous to hear stories in the biblical Book of Joshua about the Sun standing still,[25] about people walking on water, as in the Book of Matthew[26], about having water changed into wine in the Book of John[27], about a virgin birth in

---

[25]Joshua 10:12-14
[26] Matthew 14:25-31
[27] John 2:1-11

the Book of Luke[28], about a six day creation in the Book of Genesis, and about people that mysteriously appear or disappear in the books of John and Acts[29].

Not only are these stories a challenge for people to understand, but it must also bring great dismay to their very being. They might say, "Do we really have to believe this 'stuff' in order to be part of this organization?"

Many people would rather avoid the Church than embrace the words that have lost all meaning for them. Like the people in the Tower of Babel story, they no longer understand those words. They no longer buy into the dream of building a church. They walk away, seeking new ways of fulfillment.

---

[28] Luke 1:29-35
[29] John 20:19-20, John 20:26-28, Acts 5:17-24, Acts 12:5-10

Today, many churches are dealing with decreasing numbers. There are attempts to 'rearrange the deck chairs,' which brings momentary enthusiasm, but soon the same ennui sets in. The reality is that fewer and fewer people see the Church as a valid and viable option for the struggles they face in life.

Church

Every religion has some form of communal gathering. This gathering takes place in a temple, a synagogue, a mosque, a church or some other designated place of worship. As a Christian, I will focus on 'church' as the place of gathering. This ritualistic gathering is important for several reasons.

The first reason is the very nature of humanity. We are social beings. In order to develop our own story and give us a greater sense of who we are, we need the social contact of other human beings. By being in community we have a larger circle of people that care for us and a larger number of people for whom we care. By being in community we are strengthened as individuals. We are allowed to use our creative talents and abilities for the good of a larger group of people.   After family, community is an essential building block in the development of society.   Meeting together as a church allows us the opportunity to create that community.

The second reason why gathering in a worship space is important is for the sake of the ideal.   Every day we encounter a variety of things that detract us from our goals, or that inhibit our sense of well-being. In worship, we hear ancient words that remind us of aspects of life that are greater than our own existence. These words remind us of the ideals for humanity.   Therefore, within the Church, we hear stories about loving our neighbour, seeking justice for all of God's people and about caring for those who have been maligned, down-trodden, or castigated to the dung-heaps of society. Through the Church, we are given the stories of love, hope and forgiveness, as well as of possibility. Through the ideals of the Christian message, the Church reminds us of how we should live out our lives and what our priorities should be. This ideal helps us to evaluate our lives and our actions. It actually gives us *direction* for our lives.

The third reason for church attendance is the opportunity that worship provides for quiet reflection. I know there are many places that allow for quiet reflection, especially within the wonders of nature. Yet, being in church, allowing the words and the music to flow through us, over us and around us, offers moments where we can be removed from all of the busyness of the World. We all need moments during which we can hear the "still small voice" of the Holy, reminding us of who we are and of what our lives are about. In our daily living, it is too easy to lose sight of the ideal of love for all of Creation. By participating in church, we allow the solitude of quiet to invade our being and to give us a much needed break from the hectic on-goings of daily living. The quiet and solitude of the Church enables us to be strengthened, encouraged and enlivened for our journey through life.

The fourth reason that church attendance is important is because of the very words that are offered by the Church. There is so much in life that would reduce people to the role of either 'producer' or 'consumer.' With our emphasis on economic issues, we can readily see that, if we are not buying or selling, investing or spending, making or trading, we are not really living up to our economic ideals. Church reminds us that we are so much more than that! We are also loving, caring, nurturing creatures who are part of the incredible world of living things. The words within church tell us that we are loved and cared for, and that we are an integral part of all of Creation.

Within the Christian tradition, there are opportunities to confess our short-comings, our mistakes, our errors and our sins. Whether these words are spoken aloud, or whether they are prayed in silence, the reality is that we have the opportunity to reflect on our lives, to understand what we might have done wrong and to hear words of forgiveness. This is the fifth reason for church attendance.

One of the most powerful aspects of the ministry of Jesus was the words of forgiveness that he spoke. He always assured people of the opportunity to be whole, to be complete and to turn away from the actions that detracted from life. He gave them the opportunity to repent, which really means 'to turn your life in a new direction.' These words of confession and forgiveness enable us to live our lives free of guilt - joyous in the certainty that we are loved.

There are many reasons why people go to church. The five reasons I have expressed here - the importance of community, the ideal relationship for all living things, the opportunity for quiet reflection, hearing words of hope, and the realization that we are loved and forgiven - are what I wish everyone could experience within the Church of their choice.

Mission

The central part of the Christian story and the very root of the word *Christian* is the word *Christ*. The word *Christ* (or *Christos*) is the Greek word for 'messiah' or "saviour." It is this descriptor that was applied to the man named Jesus. Jesus' followers claimed that he was the messiah - the promised one of God. He was called 'the Christ.' This tells us that his disciples, his followers and the people he spoke to saw him as the one who gave life meaning and purpose. They saw him as a saviour.

The teachings of Jesus are not about following rules, other than the rule regarding the sanctity of life. Jesus put the well-being of individuals over and above the rules that are imposed by society.   Jesus was about bringing wholeness to the lives of others and about enabling others to live and to participate in life.

In the Gospel account, the true miracle is that, through his presence, Jesus was able to change the lives of people in a most dramatic fashion. The impact that Jesus had on others could be likened to receiving 650 bottles of very good wine at a wedding feast; or to becoming conscious and aware of life for the first time; or to multitudes of people all receiving sustenance for life; or to the serenity, peace and calm that can be felt after emotional, mental, or physical upheavals. These examples relate to his changing water into wine[30], raising Lazarus from death[31], feeding thousands

[30] John 2:1-11
[31] John 11:38-44

of people[32] and walking on water[33]. These stories reflect the impact he had on others. They told these stories, not as literal truth, but as metaphor and symbolism of the deep presence of love, care, nurture, justice and peace that was evident when Jesus was present.

The early followers of Jesus attempted to continue what Jesus began. They called their movement The Way[34] because they were attempting to follow in the 'way' of Jesus. They wanted to live and treat others in the same way that Jesus had. Their early days were spent sharing their resources equally with all people, bringing healing and wholeness to others, and celebrating the gifts of love and grace, which they had

[32] Matthew 14:13-21 and 15:29-39
[33] Matthew 14:22-34
[34] Acts 9:2

received. The teachings of Jesus – love, hope, grace, forgiveness, wholeness – are as valid and important today as they were two-thousand years ago.

Today, there are many people who follow the way. Many of these people are not members of a church. Doctors without Borders is one such organization. These medical specialists use their talents and abilities to assist others who are beset by drought, disease or war. In addition, most communities have resorted to 'food banks' in an effort to aid those who are in need of assistance. Many after-school programs are initiated by people who are concerned for the welfare of our children and are attempting to bring direction, love and hope into the lives of young people.

There are many people today that are enabling the teachings of Jesus to continue.   The Church should partner with all of the people who put forth his teachings in very concrete ways. But, in many cases, the Church seems to be more interested in maintaining their building,   structure,   theology,   or organization.   The Church is guilty of glorifying the messenger, rather than following   in   the   *footsteps*   of   that messenger. It is much easier to worship Jesus than it is to follow his example.

When Jesus was asked which law was most important, he replied "You must love the Most High God with all your heart, with all your soul, with all your mind and with all your strength." This teaching is at the very heart of his message.   Jesus then added that the second most important law is "You must love your neighbour as yourself."[35]

35 Mark 12:30-31

Spirit

Every day in the corner of a library in Japan an old monk was to be found sitting in peaceful meditation.

"I never see you read the sutras," said the librarian.

"I never learned to read," replied the monk.

"That's a disgrace. A monk like you ought to be able to read. Shall I teach you?"

"Yes. Tell me," said the monk, pointing to himself, "what is the meaning of this character?"

Anthony de Mello

A disciple once complained, "You tell us stories, but you never reveal their meaning to us."

Said the master, "How would you like it if someone offered you fruit and masticated it before giving it to you?"

Anthony de Mello

Introduction

The word *spirit* is a difficult word to understand. There are so many nuances and meanings for this word. I believe that we need to grasp an understanding of this word because it is at the very heart of our existence. The following examples give some ideas about the many variations of spirit that exist.

At one time, we were the proud owners of a Boston Terrier. Initially, I was surprised that this small dog had just as much "spirit of dog" as a St. Bernard or a Bernese Mountain Dog. I was also surprised by his unique personality. He had the Spirit of a Boston Terrier and yet, he had his own unique aspects – kind, feisty, proud, loving and gentle.

At some point in the very early stage of raising a newborn, young parents find out that their child has a most unique personality. The child has some of the father's traits and some of the mother's traits. But the child has a spirit that is definitely unique to him or her.

When a person enters a room, a church, or a place of business, they can sense something about that place. Most of us have encountered places that have been most welcoming and inviting. We have also been in places that gave us a sense of foreboding, a feeling of dread, or even a feeling that we were not welcome. A collection of individuals in a certain place can create some type of presence, or spirit, which can be sensed by others.

Geographically, we all have places that resonate within us. The experience of being on the prairies gives a completely different sense of self and of our world than the experience of being in the mountains. Being beside the ocean provides for quite a different experience from the experience of being beside a fast-flowing stream. Each place speaks to us and gives us a sense of calm and peace. Each place has a unique spirit that invokes a unique reaction within us.

Nations and communities develop certain attitudes and ways of existence. The unique qualities of these social structures influence people to feel either very comfortable or very ill at ease. Our existence is dependent upon being in sync with the communities in which we live. Finding a community whose spirit corresponds well with our own spirit gives us a greater sense of peace and wholeness.

The very existence of our world presupposes a certain energy or drive. That which has brought us from nothingness fourteen billion years ago, to the incredible diversity of life we have today, can be seen as some form of energy or spirit. This spirit has enabled life, in its many different forms, to evolve over the eons. It has enabled this small planet, which exists within the myriad galaxies of this vast universe, to promote life.

The following chapters touch on some aspects of spirit.

Thin Places

One of the blessings that was given to us by Celtic spirituality is the notion of 'thin places'.[36] Thin places are ordinary places that appear to have some spiritual quality within them. I have experienced places that give me a great sense of peace and wholeness, but I have also experienced activities, which create that same sense of peace and wholeness. So, in my opinion, the term should be expanded to include, not only places, but also activities.

At one time in my life, I sailed. It was an incredible experience. Indeed, it was the most religious activity that I have ever participated in. Imagine being in the middle of a body of water, with the wind and water being the dominant

---

[36] Borg, The Heart of Christianity (p.155 – 165)

powers. It was exhilarating to interact with these elements of nature. As a sailor, I had to cope with ever-changing conditions the best way I knew how. I was in the midst of something much larger and much more powerful than myself. For me, this was a thin place – a place where the Holy was very much present in the everyday.

One of my first summer jobs consisted of moving irrigation sprinkler pipes. These lines, which were connected to a larger mainline, consisted of thirty-three, four-inch aluminum pipes that measured about forty feet in length. In order to provide adequate water to the entire field, we moved the lines three times a day – at 4:00 am, at noon and again at 8:00 pm. The early morning move became my favourite time.

We began the early morning move in darkness, but soon there appeared a glowing arc on the eastern horizon. As we moved each pipe, the glowing orb would rise higher and higher in the sky. You would think that there would not be much animal life in the midst of a farmer's field on the prairies. Yet, with each pipe that was moved and, with the Sun rising higher, the entire world gradually and incessantly appeared to awaken. Soon, there was a wondrous cacophony of sound, as the animal world awoke to celebrate the new day. It was life-giving; it was energizing. Each morning, I was blessed with the holiness of a 'thin place' - a place where life was born anew every day.

I have also been blessed by having lived in Nova Scotia for ten years. While we lived in the city of Halifax, my wife and I were surrounded by locations that became thin places for us – places that transcended the ordinary. These places became places of pilgrimage.

One such place was the look-off at Herring Cove, a fishing community just outside of Halifax. While standing on the granite rocks at the look-off, watching the timeless and never-ending waves hit the shore, we felt a sense of the vastness of the world. We also felt a sense of the frailty of our human condition. It moved us to a greater appreciation for our life and our planet, and for the forces within all of Creation. It was, indeed, a thin place for us.

No matter where we travel, we encounter incredible beauty. Yet we need to reside in a place for a while in order to truly appreciate its holiness. Most people have a place of wonder, peace, beauty or serenity. These places allow us to transcend the ordinary and to sense the wonders of life and Creation.

My wife is a gardener. Thin places for most gardeners are found within the realms of annuals, perennials, fronds and shrubs. Nurturing flora becomes a thin place for them – a place where the ordinary becomes shrouded by the wonder of beauty and new life.

Everyone has their own sense of what constitutes a thin place. Upon holding their new born child, many people encounter a miracle of life – a thin place – that is both amazing and humbling.

Our world is a most remarkable place. We encounter all aspects of this world. If we allow them to, our experiences fill us with both awe and appreciation. Thin places are not unique in themselves. They *become* special because of what we bring to them. The wonder of the place, combined with our own deep sense of appreciation, helps to transform the ordinary into something extraordinary. When we sense a place as being extraordinary, it becomes a thin place, a place where we experience the holiness of life.

Our Spiritual Selves

It is my opinion that the fundamental trait for all of Creation is to nurture. This nurturing can be exchanged with all parts of Creation – plants, animals or human beings. The very dynamics of fourteen billion years of evolutionary development could only exist for one reason - the nature of the Universe is to nurture life.

Caring for newborn babies is what has allowed our species to exist. For the first years of life, babies need constant nurture, care and love. Without this nurture, our species would have died out long ago. Even when we are able to function as individuals we need the care and nurture of others. We also need to care for others. Caring for one another appears to be the fundamental basis of living. It is the constant within all of humanity.

Part of the blessings of having a pet is the opportunity to nurture and care for another living thing. Yet, in truth, the real blessing of a pet is the opportunity to receive nurture and care from this wonderful animal. Gardeners take great pleasure in nurturing and caring for their gardens. In turn, the gardener is nurtured by the beauty of plant and flower.

We are more than just a physical entity that is attempting to fulfill our bodily needs. There is a spiritual component within the reality of every person. This "spiritual component" is something that cannot be weighed, measured or defined. It is what makes each person unique. It is what causes someone to be attracted to one person and not to another, or to gravitate toward a certain activity or profession. It is what gives rise to our likes and dislikes. This spiritual component is, in essence, the very nature of our being. It is the bedrock of our existence, the reality of who we really are.

This spiritual component determines how we give and receive nurture. I would much rather have a pet than work in a garden. I am thankful that I have had the opportunity to be both a teacher, as well as being clergy. These activities have nurtured me. I would never have succeeded if I had worked in the trades or in commerce, or with technology. Nor would I have felt complete. In my opinion, my choices have provided me with the best opportunity to nurture the well-being within others, as well as to receive and nurture my own inner being. Each person needs to make the choices that nurture them and allows them to nurture others in the process.

Spiritual But Not Religious

Today, the words Spiritual But Not Religious (SBNR) are becoming quite common. Many people now describe themselves in this manner. Within the last fifty years, church attendance has decreased. But the need to nurture our inner being still remains. So people have found new and divergent ways to feed their spiritual needs.

Since the beginnings of the institution of 'church,' it has claimed and spoken for spirit. In fact, it was deemed that spirit, which is found within the Church, represented the very essence of the force/energy (God) that has given us such an abundant diversity of life.

Many church goers think that spirit does not exist outside of the Church. When churches are involved with community activities, such as food banks, some clergy stress that the work should be seen as "Christian" and that only church members should work there. Yet the very essence of spirit is something that cannot be controlled, manipulated or even adequately described. It is something that exists within each person, making them unique. Spirit exists within our world, to make it the wondrous, evolving, life-giving planet that it is.

The exodus of many people from organized church is not a reflection on the people that are leaving. The church has attempted to speak honestly about how they perceive the spiritual reality that they inherited, from the writings contained in the Bible, to the interpretations that are offered by scholars, to individual pursuits for inner peace. Knowingly or unknowingly, the Church has attempted to remain in control of spirit. Yet this quality cannot be boxed in or controlled. It cannot be under the domain of any one organization. By definition, spirit is the life-giving quality that is imbued within every living thing.

Church celebrates spirit, especially on the Sunday of Pentecost. This reading from Acts 2:1-11 gives an account of spirit. No matter what their ethnicity or language, everyone experienced something profound on the very first Pentecostal Sunday:

When the day of Pentecost arrived, they all met in one room. Suddenly they heard what sounded like a violent, rushing wind from heaven; the noise filled the entire house in which they were sitting. Something appeared to them that seemed like tongues of fire; these separated and came to rest on the head of each one. They were all filled with the Holy Spirit and began to speak in other languages as she enabled them.

Now there were devout people living in Jerusalem from every nation under heaven and at this sound they all assembled. But they were bewildered to hear their native languages being spoken. They were amazed and astonished: "Surely all of these people speaking are Galileans! How does it happen that each of us hears these words in our native tongue? We are Parthians, Medes and Elamites, people from Mesopotamia, Judea and Cappadocia, Pontus and Asia, Phrygia and Pamphylia, Egypt and the parts of Libya around Cyrene, as well as visitors from Rome – all Jews, or converts to Judaism – Cretans and Arabs, too; we hear them preaching, each in our own language, about the marvels of God![37]

---

[37] Acts 2:1-11

Today, we are experiencing a new type of Pentecost. Once again, people are hearing words that give meaning to their lives. Once again, they are experiencing the unique gifts that provide hope and nurture for their very being. Like the people in the above paragraph, the people of today are amazed that spirit can be found outside of their normal religious practices. The reality is that church is not in control of spirit.

Today, the work of church is being continued by many people around the World. The work of caring for others, enabling others and bringing justice to others is happening because people have a built in necessity to nurture and love. This is also true for the work of caring for the environment. Today, the greater community has taken up the work that the Church had been doing throughout history. The more people that are involved with the well-being of life, and of giving and receiving nurture, the more love, care and wholeness there is within our world.

A New Paradigm

Religious understanding has changed over the ages. According to our Christian history, the Israelites are credited with giving us an understanding of a God of awesome power and might. This God is beyond our understanding. They developed this belief into a religion, which has its own sets of laws and regulations. But Jesus came along and challenged those rules and regulations.

Jesus made people see that it is paramount to treat one another with respect, dignity, love and grace. It is not good enough just to follow rules and regulations, but to put what you say into action, enabling your neighbour to be loved and to be whole. Today, we have a very wide range of understandings about Jesus and religion, with every group claiming that their slant is the only correct one.

Jesus brought a new understanding to the people of his day. Likewise, Martin Luther aided in bringing a new understanding to the people of *his* day. It is my opinion that there is now a new movement happening, which brings new understanding to the people of *this* day. Every so often, there is a major change in our perspective and a great transformation takes place. I believe we are at the onset of a major change in religious understanding.

There has been a great change in the mindset of the people of this day. We can thank people like Chris Hadfield, who was the first Canadian astronaut to command the International Space Station. Chris amazed our world by bringing the reality of space travel into the homes of millions of viewers. We can thank our scientists who continually forge ahead with new discoveries. We can thank everyone who has ever brought a new and more dynamic understanding to their field of expertise, giving humanity a broader perspective of life and of religion.

In the course of life, our world and our understanding are continually evolving. Nothing remains stagnant. It grows into a new and more meaningful entity. Recognizing that, as a church, we believe strongly in spirit, we should celebrate this Spirit that is forging a new world, a new understanding and a new church.

Today, we recognize that change is happening. Unfortunately, "we see indistinctly, as in a mirror."[38] We cannot fathom the extent of change that we have yet to undergo. But, as people of faith, we can trust that the spirit, which has been present for fourteen billion years, is alive and well, and will lead us into new ways of being.

Enabling Love

When I was growing up, I often heard the expression "they are so heavenly minded they are no earthly good." This was generally said about a person who spent too much time within church, or who was focused only on ideas within the Bible. They became completely myopic to the World around them. In fact, the reality of community took a backseat to what they believed was going to be their "just reward."

One of the largest negatives within all religions is the erroneous belief that participating in religious activities prepares us for the next life. Religious extremists, who initiate hatred and killing because they think it will bring them into a glorious next life, have lost sight of what it means to care for one's neighbour. Within Christian circles, there are people who believe that their church attendance, tithing, prayer and bible study will assure them of a place at the "banquet table" of God and Jesus in the hereafter.

When I read the Gospels, I encounter a Jesus who attempted to bring people into community. When a person who was suffering from leprosy was isolated, alone and unable to interact with others, it was Jesus' healing that allowed them to function within society once again. When it was told that Jesus walked on water, this was a symbolic account of how Jesus was able to overcome the upheavals and turmoil of life. When Jesus fed the multitudes, this was a symbolic gesture to show us that everyone is important and is welcome to a loving and nurturing life.

The stories of Jesus remind us that it is the "here and now" in which we live. It is only in the present time and within our own communities that we exist. We need to focus on the "here and now," not on something we have no control over.

The focus on the afterlife divides the World into two camps – "the chosen" and "the damned." The unfortunate result is that we always put ourselves into the chosen camp (no matter what our beliefs), while we always place those who differ from us into the camp of the damned (no matter what their beliefs).

There are many stories about people who have had a Near Death Experience (NDE). I want to honor those stories. However, I wish to caution people not to live solely for the next life but, rather, to be involved in this life as much as possible. It should be noted that many of the stories about NDEs happen to people who have no involvement with organized religion. However, through their experiences, they end up having an incredible sense of the Holy.

One such person was Eben Alexander, the author of a book entitled *Proof of Heaven*. He maintains that, while he experienced his NDE, he sensed that he was being imparted with phenomenal knowledge. The message he received was, "You are loved and cherished. You have nothing to fear. There is nothing you can do wrong." He goes on to state that, if he were to boil this message down to its simplest form, it would only be "love." [39] He expands on this by stressing that love is at the very

---

[39] Alexander, Proof of Heaven, p. 71

core of our existence. He describes this love as being the very essence of life:

In its purest and most powerful form, this love is not jealous or selfish, but unconditional. This is the reality of realities, the incomprehensibly glorious truth of truths that lives and breathes at the core of everything that exists or that ever will exist and no remotely accurate understanding of who and what we are can be achieved by anyone who does not know it and embody it in all of their actions.[40]

At the beginning of this book, I spoke of God as being a 'nurturing presence.' There is a mysterious energy that is pulsating through our world – one that has caused us to continuously develop for fourteen billion years. This energy has been called many names,

---

[40] Ibid, p. 71

God being one of them. The experiences of people, such as Eben Alexander, suggest that this pulsating energy is forever nurturing, caring and recreating our world. It is this reality (which can never be controlled by any one person or organization) that nurtures life, creates unique understandings and continually proliferates the World with wondrous diversity. It is this very energy and drive that is bringing change to our churches and to our very world.

Honoring our Spirit

Our bodies are made up of cells. These cells enable our bodies to grow, develop and change. Occasionally, cells appear to be bent, not on enabling life, but on destroying the very life that enables them to exist. Cells like these are cancerous. To rid itself of these rogue cells, the body must go through vigorous struggles.

This is a meaningful metaphor for our world. Each individual is a cell. Most people in the World are here to enable, develop and support life. However there are also rogue cells in the World. These are the individuals that are bent on destroying the life that supports them.

This challenges us in many ways. First, we need to see how we allow the life-giving qualities to permeate our very being. Recognizing that we are not just a physical entity, but also a spiritual being, we need to feed and nurture that spirit. How do we allow our spirit to be rejuvenated? How do we step away from the busyness of life so that we can reassess our energy, our priorities and our very lives? How can we turn off the voices of the people who diminish us, that make us feel small or insignificant, or that demean us? It is my hope that everyone will be able to say a resounding 'yes' to the very unique individual that they are and to celebrate themselves as a gift to the Universe!

The second way in which we are challenged is to honor our very self, by protecting it from people who attempt to destroy the Spirit that makes each one of us unique and special. There are rogue cells (individuals) that seek out people that they can use for their own gains, enslaving them for drugs, sex or power. These are the people who willingly sacrifice the life of another person for their own well-being. They care not a whit for the well-being of others. The Easter story of Jesus being arrested, tried, and then executed is a story of the Chief Priests and Elders who willingly sacrificed an innocent man in order to hold on to their power.

Many of these rogue cells prey on the misery of others, seeking out the abused, the poor, the hurt and the lonely, in order to carry out their nefarious activities for selfish ambition. Unfortunately, these types of people can be found within legitimate organizations, such as churches, governments and businesses. It is here that they cover up their selfish schemes, by cloaking them in the robe of respectability. It is our duty to protect our spirits from the very people who want to destroy the uniqueness of our being.

The third way in which we are challenged is in seeing how our actions affect the lives of all other living things. In order for humanity to survive on planet Earth, we need to care for all other species. Without the rest of life, human beings would soon become extinct. What kind of footprint are we leaving on our world? The work we do, the things we buy, the food we eat and how we live say something about our effect on the rest of life. Are our lives enabling others to live? Could it be that humanity is really the rogue cells within the whole of Creation?

In the beginning of this book, I spoke of God as being a life-giving energy. Every living thing has within it that spiritual force. We are part of that spirit. We are a part of that life-force that is called God. We must honor the Spirit that is within us, as well as the Spirit that is within all living things.

Epilogue

Human beings have an innate curiosity about life. Our journey through life is always about asking questions. The field of science is proof of this. Scientists, in whatever field, continually push against the unknown. We, the ordinary folk, may not have the skills or tools that are used by scientists, but we too are continually probing the mysteries of our life and of our existence. Through the passage of time, we begin to realize that the answers we had previously embraced now appear to be simplistic and shallow. The faith journey is a wonderful example of this.

While we were very young, many of us who were raised in the Church were taught about God and how this power had created us, watched over us and loved us. As we aged, we began to question the idea of the grandfather figure that was sitting in some nebulous place, called Heaven, watching over us and smiling, or shaking a finger at our antics. It appears that Christians have chosen three different directions in which to continue their search for meaning.

For some Christians, the questions and the questioning were simply wrong. People were expected to believe exactly what was said about God, embracing what they were taught, without question.

Other Christians ended up saying, "This God stuff just doesn't make any sense." They jettisoned the whole package of Christianity.

Still another group of Christians began to recognize the deeper meaning behind the words and the stories. This third group attempts to see both life and spirit as a dynamic, ever-evolving, life-giving energy.

Dairmuid O'Murchu is a priest, a social psychologist and the author of a book entitled *Quantum Theology*. He sees this energy/power as spirit. He describes the spiritual work, both past and present, in this illuminating paragraph:

Christian missionaries often remark that the spirit leads people to Christ, a statement made with the underlying assumption that only toward the Christ of Christianity can the spirit lead. For several millennia, however, the spirit has led people to a sense of holy mystery, long before the Christian religion ever evolved. We need to be wary and much more discerning lest our Christian ideology (an imperialism) leads us away from deeper truth rather than toward it. Assuredly, the spirit leads people in ways we can only discern with hindsight and in retrospect. It may or may not be toward the Christian Christ, but consistently it will be to energize and empower people toward a fuller and deeper sense of our sacred humanity, as well as a deeper recognition of the sacred at work in every sphere of God's creation.[41]

Our universe, our planet, indeed our very life, is filled with spirit. This is not some vague theological assumption. It is a truth that is seen in the life of every living thing. We see it in plants, animals, human beings and within all of Creation. The energy/power/spirit that is propelling all of life forward is the very spirit that enables us to breathe, to laugh and to celebrate life.

Life is filled with awe and wonder. My prayer for you, the reader, is to never

---

[41] O'Murchu, <u>In the Beginning Was the spirit</u>, p. 100

let go of your desire for answers. Continue to probe the mysteries of life. Allow the wonders of Creation, the wonders of spirit, to fill you with appreciation for this incredible gift of life. Never allow anyone to diminish your light, or the light of the Divine, which radiates through every aspect of our universe.

Thanks be to the Divine!

Bibliography

Alexander, Eben. Proof of Heaven. 2012. New York: Simon and Schuster, Inc.

Armstrong, Karen. The Case for God. 2009. Toronto: Alfred A. Knopf.

Barnett, Kristine. The Spark. Toronto: 2013. Random House Canada.

Borg, Marcus J. The Heart of Christianity. 2003. New York: HarperCollins Publishers Inc.

deMello, Anthony, S.J. Taking Flight. 1990. New York: An Image Book.

deMello, Anthony, S.J. The Song of the Bird. 1984. New York: An Image Book.

Dowd, Michael. Thank God for Evolution. 2009. New York: A Plume Book.

Harper, Tom. The Pagan Christ. Toronto: 2004. Thomas Allen Publishers.

Achtemeier, Paul. Harper's Bible
Dictionary. 1985. United States:
Harper, San Francisco.

Priests for Equality. The Inclusive Bible:
The First Egalitarian Translation 2007.
United Kingdom: Rowman & Littlefield
Publishers, Inc.

Krauss, Lawrence M. A Universe From
Nothing. 2012. New York: Atria
Paperback.

Fox, Matthew. Meditations with Meister
Eckhart. 1983. Santa Fe: Bear &
Company.

Brown, Raymond Edward. New Jerome
Biblical Commentary. 1991. Avon,
Great Britain: Bath Press

O'Murchu, Diarmuid. Quantum
Theology. 2004. New York: Crossroad
Publishing Company.

_____. In the Beginning
Was the Spirit. 2012. New York: Orbis
Books